DATE / TIME	Oil Changed	Air Filter	Rotate/Balance Tires	Tire Replaced	Wheel Alignment	Fuel Filter	Brakes Serviced	Spark Plugs	Transmission	Wiper Blades	Batteries	Radiator	Belts & Hoses	MILEAGE

OTHER MAINTENANCE

DATE / TIME	*DESCRIPTION*	*MILEAGE*

DATE / TIME	Oil Changed	Air Filter	Rotate/Balance Tires	Tire Replaced	Wheel Alignment	Fuel Filter	Brakes Serviced	Spark Plugs	Transmission	Wiper Blades	Batteries	Radiator	Belts & Hoses	*MILEAGE*

OTHER MAINTENANCE

DATE / TIME	DESCRIPTION	MILEAGE

DATE / TIME	Oil Changed	Air Filter	Rotate/Balance Tires	Tire Replaced	Wheel Alignment	Fuel Filter	Brakes Serviced	Spark Plugs	Transmission	Wiper Blades	Batteries	Radiator	Belts & Hoses	*MILEAGE*

OTHER MAINTENANCE

DATE / TIME	*DESCRIPTION*	*MILEAGE*

DATE / TIME	Oil Changed	Air Filter	Rotate/Balance Tires	Tire Replaced	Wheel Alignment	Fuel Filter	Brakes Serviced	Spark Plugs	Transmission	Wiper Blades	Batteries	Radiator	Belts & Hoses	*MILEAGE*

OTHER MAINTENANCE

DATE / TIME	DESCRIPTION	MILEAGE

DATE / TIME	Oil Changed	Air Filter	Rotate/Balance Tires	Tire Replaced	Wheel Alignment	Fuel Filter	Brakes Serviced	Spark Plugs	Transmission	Wiper Blades	Batteries	Radiator	Belts & Hoses	*MILEAGE*

OTHER MAINTENANCE

DATE / TIME	*DESCRIPTION*	*MILEAGE*

DATE / TIME	Oil Changed	Air Filter	Rotate/Balance Tires	Tire Replaced	Wheel Alignment	Fuel Filter	Brakes Serviced	Spark Plugs	Transmission	Wiper Blades	Batteries	Radiator	Belts & Hoses	***MILEAGE***

OTHER MAINTENANCE

DATE / TIME	DESCRIPTION	MILEAGE

DATE / TIME	Oil Changed	Air Filter	Rotate/Balance Tires	Tire Replaced	Wheel Alignment	Fuel Filter	Brakes Serviced	Spark Plugs	Transmission	Wiper Blades	Batteries	Radiator	Belts & Hoses	*MILEAGE*

OTHER MAINTENANCE

DATE / TIME	*DESCRIPTION*	*MILEAGE*

DATE / TIME	Oil Changed	Air Filter	Rotate/Balance Tires	Tire Replaced	Wheel Alignment	Fuel Filter	Brakes Serviced	Spark Plugs	Transmission	Wiper Blades	Batteries	Radiator	Belts & Hoses	*MILEAGE*

OTHER MAINTENANCE

DATE / TIME	*DESCRIPTION*	*MILEAGE*

DATE / TIME	Oil Changed	Air Filter	Rotate/Balance Tires	Tire Replaced	Wheel Alignment	Fuel Filter	Brakes Serviced	Spark Plugs	Transmission	Wiper Blades	Batteries	Radiator	Belts & Hoses	*MILEAGE*

OTHER MAINTENANCE

DATE / TIME	DESCRIPTION	MILEAGE

DATE / TIME	Oil Changed	Air Filter	Rotate/Balance Tires	Tire Replaced	Wheel Alignment	Fuel Filter	Brakes Serviced	Spark Plugs	Transmission	Wiper Blades	Batteries	Radiator	Belts & Hoses	***MILEAGE***

OTHER MAINTENANCE

DATE / TIME	*DESCRIPTION*	*MILEAGE*

DATE / TIME	Oil Changed	Air Filter	Rotate/Balance Tires	Tire Replaced	Wheel Alignment	Fuel Filter	Brakes Serviced	Spark Plugs	Transmission	Wiper Blades	Batteries	Radiator	Belts & Hoses	*MILEAGE*

OTHER MAINTENANCE

DATE / TIME	DESCRIPTION	MILEAGE

DATE / TIME	Oil Changed	Air Filter	Rotate/Balance Tires	Tire Replaced	Wheel Alignment	Fuel Filter	Brakes Serviced	Spark Plugs	Transmission	Wiper Blades	Batteries	Radiator	Belts & Hoses	MILEAGE

OTHER MAINTENANCE

DATE / TIME	DESCRIPTION	MILEAGE

DATE / TIME	Oil Changed	Air Filter	Rotate/Balance Tires	Tire Replaced	Wheel Alignment	Fuel Filter	Brakes Serviced	Spark Plugs	Transmission	Wiper Blades	Batteries	Radiator	Belts & Hoses	*MILEAGE*

OTHER MAINTENANCE

DATE / TIME	*DESCRIPTION*	*MILEAGE*

DATE / TIME	Oil Changed	Air Filter	Rotate/Balance Tires	Tire Replaced	Wheel Alignment	Fuel Filter	Brakes Serviced	Spark Plugs	Transmission	Wiper Blades	Batteries	Radiator	Belts & Hoses	*MILEAGE*

OTHER MAINTENANCE

DATE / TIME	DESCRIPTION	MILEAGE

DATE / TIME	Oil Changed	Air Filter	Rotate/Balance Tires	Tire Replaced	Wheel Alignment	Fuel Filter	Brakes Serviced	Spark Plugs	Transmission	Wiper Blades	Batteries	Radiator	Belts & Hoses	MILEAGE

OTHER MAINTENANCE

DATE / TIME	*DESCRIPTION*	*MILEAGE*

DATE / TIME	Oil Changed	Air Filter	Rotate/Balance Tires	Tire Replaced	Wheel Alignment	Fuel Filter	Brakes Serviced	Spark Plugs	Transmission	Wiper Blades	Batteries	Radiator	Belts & Hoses	*MILEAGE*

OTHER MAINTENANCE

DATE / TIME	*DESCRIPTION*	*MILEAGE*

DATE / TIME	Oil Changed	Air Filter	Rotate/Balance Tires	Tire Replaced	Wheel Alignment	Fuel Filter	Brakes Serviced	Spark Plugs	Transmission	Wiper Blades	Batteries	Radiator	Belts & Hoses	*MILEAGE*

OTHER MAINTENANCE

DATE / TIME	DESCRIPTION	MILEAGE

DATE / TIME	Oil Changed	Air Filter	Rotate/Balance Tires	Tire Replaced	Wheel Alignment	Fuel Filter	Brakes Serviced	Spark Plugs	Transmission	Wiper Blades	Batteries	Radiator	Belts & Hoses	*MILEAGE*

OTHER MAINTENANCE

DATE / TIME	*DESCRIPTION*	*MILEAGE*

DATE / TIME	Oil Changed	Air Filter	Rotate/Balance Tires	Tire Replaced	Wheel Alignment	Fuel Filter	Brakes Serviced	Spark Plugs	Transmission	Wiper Blades	Batteries	Radiator	Belts & Hoses	MILEAGE

OTHER MAINTENANCE

DATE / TIME	*DESCRIPTION*	*MILEAGE*

DATE / TIME	Oil Changed	Air Filter	Rotate/Balance Tires	Tire Replaced	Wheel Alignment	Fuel Filter	Brakes Serviced	Spark Plugs	Transmission	Wiper Blades	Batteries	Radiator	Belts & Hoses	*MILEAGE*

OTHER MAINTENANCE

DATE / TIME	DESCRIPTION	MILEAGE

DATE / TIME	Oil Changed	Air Filter	Rotate/Balance Tires	Tire Replaced	Wheel Alignment	Fuel Filter	Brakes Serviced	Spark Plugs	Transmission	Wiper Blades	Batteries	Radiator	Belts & Hoses	MILEAGE

OTHER MAINTENANCE

DATE / TIME	DESCRIPTION	MILEAGE

DATE / TIME	Oil Changed	Air Filter	Rotate/Balance Tires	Tire Replaced	Wheel Alignment	Fuel Filter	Brakes Serviced	Spark Plugs	Transmission	Wiper Blades	Batteries	Radiator	Belts & Hoses	***MILEAGE***

OTHER MAINTENANCE

DATE / TIME	*DESCRIPTION*	*MILEAGE*

DATE / TIME	Oil Changed	Air Filter	Rotate/Balance Tires	Tire Replaced	Wheel Alignment	Fuel Filter	Brakes Serviced	Spark Plugs	Transmission	Wiper Blades	Batteries	Radiator	Belts & Hoses	*MILEAGE*

OTHER MAINTENANCE

DATE / TIME	*DESCRIPTION*	*MILEAGE*

DATE / TIME	Oil Changed	Air Filter	Rotate/Balance Tires	Tire Replaced	Wheel Alignment	Fuel Filter	Brakes Serviced	Spark Plugs	Transmission	Wiper Blades	Batteries	Radiator	Belts & Hoses	*MILEAGE*

OTHER MAINTENANCE

DATE / TIME	*DESCRIPTION*	*MILEAGE*

DATE / TIME	Oil Changed	Air Filter	Rotate/Balance Tires	Tire Replaced	Wheel Alignment	Fuel Filter	Brakes Serviced	Spark Plugs	Transmission	Wiper Blades	Batteries	Radiator	Belts & Hoses	***MILEAGE***

OTHER MAINTENANCE

DATE / TIME	*DESCRIPTION*	*MILEAGE*

DATE / TIME	Oil Changed	Air Filter	Rotate/Balance Tires	Tire Replaced	Wheel Alignment	Fuel Filter	Brakes Serviced	Spark Plugs	Transmission	Wiper Blades	Batteries	Radiator	Belts & Hoses	*MILEAGE*

OTHER MAINTENANCE

DATE / TIME	DESCRIPTION	MILEAGE

DATE / TIME	Oil Changed	Air Filter	Rotate/Balance Tires	Tire Replaced	Wheel Alignment	Fuel Filter	Brakes Serviced	Spark Plugs	Transmission	Wiper Blades	Batteries	Radiator	Belts & Hoses	*MILEAGE*

OTHER MAINTENANCE

DATE / TIME	*DESCRIPTION*	*MILEAGE*

DATE / TIME	Oil Changed	Air Filter	Rotate/Balance Tires	Tire Replaced	Wheel Alignment	Fuel Filter	Brakes Serviced	Spark Plugs	Transmission	Wiper Blades	Batteries	Radiator	Belts & Hoses	MILEAGE

OTHER MAINTENANCE

DATE / TIME	*DESCRIPTION*	*MILEAGE*

DATE / TIME	Oil Changed	Air Filter	Rotate/Balance Tires	Tire Replaced	Wheel Alignment	Fuel Filter	Brakes Serviced	Spark Plugs	Transmission	Wiper Blades	Batteries	Radiator	Belts & Hoses	***MILEAGE***

OTHER MAINTENANCE

DATE / TIME	*DESCRIPTION*	*MILEAGE*

DATE / TIME	Oil Changed	Air Filter	Rotate/Balance Tires	Tire Replaced	Wheel Alignment	Fuel Filter	Brakes Serviced	Spark Plugs	Transmission	Wiper Blades	Batteries	Radiator	Belts & Hoses	*MILEAGE*

OTHER MAINTENANCE

DATE / TIME	DESCRIPTION	MILEAGE

DATE / TIME	Oil Changed	Air Filter	Rotate/Balance Tires	Tire Replaced	Wheel Alignment	Fuel Filter	Brakes Serviced	Spark Plugs	Transmission	Wiper Blades	Batteries	Radiator	Belts & Hoses	*MILEAGE*

OTHER MAINTENANCE

DATE / TIME	*DESCRIPTION*	*MILEAGE*

DATE / TIME	Oil Changed	Air Filter	Rotate/Balance Tires	Tire Replaced	Wheel Alignment	Fuel Filter	Brakes Serviced	Spark Plugs	Transmission	Wiper Blades	Batteries	Radiator	Belts & Hoses	*MILEAGE*

OTHER MAINTENANCE

DATE / TIME	*DESCRIPTION*	*MILEAGE*

DATE / TIME	Oil Changed	Air Filter	Rotate/Balance Tires	Tire Replaced	Wheel Alignment	Fuel Filter	Brakes Serviced	Spark Plugs	Transmission	Wiper Blades	Batteries	Radiator	Belts & Hoses	***MILEAGE***

OTHER MAINTENANCE

DATE / TIME	*DESCRIPTION*	*MILEAGE*

DATE / TIME	Oil Changed	Air Filter	Rotate/Balance Tires	Tire Replaced	Wheel Alignment	Fuel Filter	Brakes Serviced	Spark Plugs	Transmission	Wiper Blades	Batteries	Radiator	Belts & Hoses	*MILEAGE*

OTHER MAINTENANCE

DATE / TIME	*DESCRIPTION*	*MILEAGE*

DATE / TIME	Oil Changed	Air Filter	Rotate/Balance Tires	Tire Replaced	Wheel Alignment	Fuel Filter	Brakes Serviced	Spark Plugs	Transmission	Wiper Blades	Batteries	Radiator	Belts & Hoses	*MILEAGE*

OTHER MAINTENANCE

DATE / TIME	*DESCRIPTION*	*MILEAGE*

DATE / TIME	Oil Changed	Air Filter	Rotate/Balance Tires	Tire Replaced	Wheel Alignment	Fuel Filter	Brakes Serviced	Spark Plugs	Transmission	Wiper Blades	Batteries	Radiator	Belts & Hoses	*MILEAGE*

OTHER MAINTENANCE

DATE / TIME	*DESCRIPTION*	*MILEAGE*

DATE / TIME	Oil Changed	Air Filter	Rotate/Balance Tires	Tire Replaced	Wheel Alignment	Fuel Filter	Brakes Serviced	Spark Plugs	Transmission	Wiper Blades	Batteries	Radiator	Belts & Hoses	*MILEAGE*

OTHER MAINTENANCE

DATE / TIME	*DESCRIPTION*	*MILEAGE*

DATE / TIME	Oil Changed	Air Filter	Rotate/Balance Tires	Tire Replaced	Wheel Alignment	Fuel Filter	Brakes Serviced	Spark Plugs	Transmission	Wiper Blades	Batteries	Radiator	Belts & Hoses	*MILEAGE*

OTHER MAINTENANCE

DATE / TIME	*DESCRIPTION*	*MILEAGE*

DATE / TIME	Oil Changed	Air Filter	Rotate/Balance Tires	Tire Replaced	Wheel Alignment	Fuel Filter	Brakes Serviced	Spark Plugs	Transmission	Wiper Blades	Batteries	Radiator	Belts & Hoses	*MILEAGE*

OTHER MAINTENANCE

DATE / TIME	DESCRIPTION	MILEAGE

DATE / TIME	Oil Changed	Air Filter	Rotate/Balance Tires	Tire Replaced	Wheel Alignment	Fuel Filter	Brakes Serviced	Spark Plugs	Transmission	Wiper Blades	Batteries	Radiator	Belts & Hoses	*MILEAGE*

OTHER MAINTENANCE

DATE / TIME	*DESCRIPTION*	*MILEAGE*

DATE / TIME	Oil Changed	Air Filter	Rotate/Balance Tires	Tire Replaced	Wheel Alignment	Fuel Filter	Brakes Serviced	Spark Plugs	Transmission	Wiper Blades	Batteries	Radiator	Belts & Hoses	*MILEAGE*

OTHER MAINTENANCE

DATE / TIME	*DESCRIPTION*	*MILEAGE*

DATE / TIME	Oil Changed	Air Filter	Rotate/Balance Tires	Tire Replaced	Wheel Alignment	Fuel Filter	Brakes Serviced	Spark Plugs	Transmission	Wiper Blades	Batteries	Radiator	Belts & Hoses	*MILEAGE*

OTHER MAINTENANCE

DATE / TIME	*DESCRIPTION*	*MILEAGE*

DATE / TIME	Oil Changed	Air Filter	Rotate/Balance Tires	Tire Replaced	Wheel Alignment	Fuel Filter	Brakes Serviced	Spark Plugs	Transmission	Wiper Blades	Batteries	Radiator	Belts & Hoses	*MILEAGE*

OTHER MAINTENANCE

DATE / TIME	*DESCRIPTION*	*MILEAGE*

DATE / TIME	Oil Changed	Air Filter	Rotate/Balance Tires	Tire Replaced	Wheel Alignment	Fuel Filter	Brakes Serviced	Spark Plugs	Transmission	Wiper Blades	Batteries	Radiator	Belts & Hoses	***MILEAGE***

OTHER MAINTENANCE

DATE / TIME	DESCRIPTION	MILEAGE

DATE / TIME	Oil Changed	Air Filter	Rotate/Balance Tires	Tire Replaced	Wheel Alignment	Fuel Filter	Brakes Serviced	Spark Plugs	Transmission	Wiper Blades	Batteries	Radiator	Belts & Hoses	MILEAGE

OTHER MAINTENANCE

DATE / TIME	*DESCRIPTION*	*MILEAGE*

DATE / TIME	Oil Changed	Air Filter	Rotate/Balance Tires	Tire Replaced	Wheel Alignment	Fuel Filter	Brakes Serviced	Spark Plugs	Transmission	Wiper Blades	Batteries	Radiator	Belts & Hoses	*MILEAGE*

OTHER MAINTENANCE

DATE / TIME	*DESCRIPTION*	*MILEAGE*

DATE / TIME	Oil Changed	Air Filter	Rotate/Balance Tires	Tire Replaced	Wheel Alignment	Fuel Filter	Brakes Serviced	Spark Plugs	Transmission	Wiper Blades	Batteries	Radiator	Belts & Hoses	*MILEAGE*

OTHER MAINTENANCE

DATE / TIME	*DESCRIPTION*	*MILEAGE*

DATE / TIME	Oil Changed	Air Filter	Rotate/Balance Tires	Tire Replaced	Wheel Alignment	Fuel Filter	Brakes Serviced	Spark Plugs	Transmission	Wiper Blades	Batteries	Radiator	Belts & Hoses	*MILEAGE*

OTHER MAINTENANCE

DATE / TIME	DESCRIPTION	MILEAGE

DATE / TIME	Oil Changed	Air Filter	Rotate/Balance Tires	Tire Replaced	Wheel Alignment	Fuel Filter	Brakes Serviced	Spark Plugs	Transmission	Wiper Blades	Batteries	Radiator	Belts & Hoses	***MILEAGE***

OTHER MAINTENANCE

DATE / TIME	*DESCRIPTION*	*MILEAGE*

DATE / TIME	Oil Changed	Air Filter	Rotate/Balance Tires	Tire Replaced	Wheel Alignment	Fuel Filter	Brakes Serviced	Spark Plugs	Transmission	Wiper Blades	Batteries	Radiator	Belts & Hoses	MILEAGE

OTHER MAINTENANCE

DATE / TIME	*DESCRIPTION*	*MILEAGE*

DATE / TIME	Oil Changed	Air Filter	Rotate/Balance Tires	Tire Replaced	Wheel Alignment	Fuel Filter	Brakes Serviced	Spark Plugs	Transmission	Wiper Blades	Batteries	Radiator	Belts & Hoses	*MILEAGE*

OTHER MAINTENANCE

DATE / TIME	*DESCRIPTION*	*MILEAGE*

DATE / TIME	Oil Changed	Air Filter	Rotate/Balance Tires	Tire Replaced	Wheel Alignment	Fuel Filter	Brakes Serviced	Spark Plugs	Transmission	Wiper Blades	Batteries	Radiator	Belts & Hoses	MILEAGE

OTHER MAINTENANCE

DATE / TIME	DESCRIPTION	MILEAGE

DATE / TIME	Oil Changed	Air Filter	Rotate/Balance Tires	Tire Replaced	Wheel Alignment	Fuel Filter	Brakes Serviced	Spark Plugs	Transmission	Wiper Blades	Batteries	Radiator	Belts & Hoses	*MILEAGE*

OTHER MAINTENANCE

DATE / TIME	DESCRIPTION	MILEAGE

DATE / TIME	Oil Changed	Air Filter	Rotate/Balance Tires	Tire Replaced	Wheel Alignment	Fuel Filter	Brakes Serviced	Spark Plugs	Transmission	Wiper Blades	Batteries	Radiator	Belts & Hoses	*MILEAGE*

OTHER MAINTENANCE

DATE / TIME	*DESCRIPTION*	*MILEAGE*

		Ai…	Rotate/… Tires	Tire Replaced	Wheel Alignment	Fuel Filter	Brakes Serviced	Spark Plugs	Transmission	Wiper Blades	Batteries	Radiator	Belts & Hoses	***MILEAGE***

OTHER MAINTENANCE

DATE / TIME	DESCRIPTION	MILEAGE

DATE / TIME	Oil Changed	Air Filter	Rotate/Balance Tires	Tire Replaced	Wheel Alignment	Fuel Filter	Brakes Serviced	Spark Plugs	Transmission	Wiper Blades	Batteries	Radiator	Belts & Hoses	*MILEAGE*

OTHER MAINTENANCE

DATE / TIME	DESCRIPTION	MILEAGE

DATE / TIME	Oil Changed	Air Filter	Rotate/Balance Tires	Tire Replaced	Wheel Alignment	Fuel Filter	Brakes Serviced	Spark Plugs	Transmission	Wiper Blades	Batteries	Radiator	Belts & Hoses	*MILEAGE*

OTHER MAINTENANCE

DATE / TIME	*DESCRIPTION*	*MILEAGE*

DATE / TIME	Oil Changed	Air Filter	Rotate/Balance Tires	Tire Replaced	Wheel Alignment	Fuel Filter	Brakes Serviced	Spark Plugs	Transmission	Wiper Blades	Batteries	Radiator	Belts & Hoses	*MILEAGE*

OTHER MAINTENANCE

DATE / TIME	*DESCRIPTION*	*MILEAGE*

DATE / TIME	Oil Changed	Air Filter	Rotate/Balance Tires	Tire Replaced	Wheel Alignment	Fuel Filter	Brakes Serviced	Spark Plugs	Transmission	Wiper Blades	Batteries	Radiator	Belts & Hoses	*MILEAGE*

OTHER MAINTENANCE

DATE / TIME	*DESCRIPTION*	*MILEAGE*

Made in the USA
Monee, IL
05 October 2022

15309449R00069